Calligraphy:

Lessons For Beginners

Disclamer: All photos used in this book, including the cover photo were made available under a Attribution-NonCommercial-ShareAlike 2.0 Generic and sourced from Flickr

Table of content

Introduction

You wander through the card selection at the store, trying to pick out that perfect one for the occasion that is coming up. You know just what you want to say, but there doesn't seem to be a card available that is going to say what you need it to.

Sure, you can go home and write it all out yourself, but you want it to be nice, to be special, and your common handwriting that you can barely read on a good day isn't exactly going to cut it for what you want it for. So what are you going to do?

If you could write like they do in the cards then you would be fine. All of your problems would be solved, and you could make your own card for any occasion. It would eliminate anymore need to wander in and out of the Hallmark stores, trying to find that one card for that one person.

If you were able to write it like that, you would have all your gift needs covered, your journal would become a work of art, and you would be free to have your cards say what you want them to say, every time, no more questions asked.

But that is where the trick is. How are you going to learn how to write like that? It looks like something Shakespeare himself would have written, with all of those fancy, even swoops and dashes. When you try it you end up with oversized letters in the beginning and smaller letters at the end.

Or you may find that it is a lot harder than it looks to make those letters make those swoops and still connect at the end where they ought to. But now, your problems are solved.

I am going to teach you how to make those calligraphy letters, and show you how you can put them on your own cards. No matter what you want to say or who you want to say it to, you now have a fancy and elegant way to do it.

You don't ever need to worry about the cards that aren't quite right, or getting the same card that someone else did. When you can make it yourself, you can make it completely custom from you and for the person you are making it for.

This is a frustrating skill to learn when you don't have a guide, but now that you have this book, you are going to learn just how easy it is to make beautiful letters, no matter where you need them to be.

So what are you waiting for?

There is a scribe inside of you, just waiting to be let out.

Chapter 1 – Getting Started

I know you are eager to begin, but it is important that we start at the beginning to ensure that you have everything that you need, as well as the beginning skills that you are going to need to practice.

Calligraphy can be a little pricey to get in to, but if you are patient, or if you are willing to start small, you are going to be able to get enough to get started in the hobby without much difficulty.

Most craft stores carry all of the things you are going to need, and if you don't like going out, you can always use the internet to order what you want. Make sure you are ordering what is for beginners. I know it sounds more fun to go with the big leagues on the outset, but I promise you that you are going to have better results if you are starting out where you should.

There is no shame in starting in the beginner realm. This is where things are going to be easier for you to get the hang of, and once you have your skills sharpened, you are going to be ready to move on.

Calligraphy is like any other hobby, the more you work at it, the better you are going to get at it. Be persistent and be patient, and you are going to get to where you want to be in no time at all.

What you will need

Here are the things you are going to need to get started. Of course, the options within these categories are boundless, so you can shop around and get anything as fancy or as simple as you would like, but anything that is meant for a beginner is going to do the trick for you.

- A pen

  There are all kinds of options for calligraphy pens. At a craft store, odds are you are going to find some pretty basic pens, and many that are made for the beginner.

  If you happen to get a pen that is filled with ink already, you are ready to go, all you will need is paper. They do make and sell quite a few like this these days, but there are some people that still prefer the older dip pen method.

  Choose what works best for you, and you are set.

- Ink

  If you decide to use the standard dip pen, then you are going to need to purchase some ink. Ink is really easy to buy, and all you really need to do is pick the color that you prefer.

  I suggest you start with black or something dark, in the standard ink. You don't want to get too fancy on the outset, as some inks are harder to work with than others, and you are going to have a harder time with them.

- Paper

  Use paper that is lined and meant for calligraphy. Again, this can be purchased at the craft store, and you won't have much difficulty deciding what you are going to need.

  This is paper that isn't going to let the ink bleed, and it is usually lined so you can practice with the letters in the appropriate place. I highly recommend that you use lined paper on the outset, then go for the blank paper later on.

- Cleaner (optional)

Ink pens that are dipped need to be cleaned. You can use nail polish remover, hot soapy water, or an ink cleaner. The ink cleaner is sold along with the inks in most craft stores.

- Cleaning pad (optional)

Again, this is optional, but it makes cleaning your pen a lot easier than just a dip cleaner.

Starting with the basics

I know right now you want to be making those large, swooping letters that cover a page all on their own, and I promise you are going to get there eventually, but you are going to need to build up to that point.

In the beginning, you are going to have to stay small. Look online for the alphabet guides, and you are going to have your pick of the crop. There are countless different styles and fonts to choose from, and it all comes down to which one you like better.

Start small, and confidently. Of course you aren't going to be as good as you would like to be at first, but you are going to have to learn how to be confident in your strokes. Make them like you mean them, and even if they aren't quite right, you are going to be able to see a deliberation in them that you will want to see in your perfected lettering.

Anyone can tell when they look at your work if you were confident in your strokes, or if your hand was shaking, and if you are dealing with a shaking hand, your work is going to reflect that.

Make your letters with confidence, and let that confidence shine forth.

Practice makes perfect

I can't emphasize enough how important it is for you to practice the letters you choose. The more you work at it, the better it is going to be, hands down. I want you to enjoy your work, and I want you to love how it turns out, the more you practice, the more you are going to like it.

Practice proper form, and holding your pen properly, and practice making the strokes even and complete in one try. You are going to have to work at this, but you will pick up on it soon enough.

Keep at it, using a mirror if you want to make sure you are at the right form, and make your mark like you mean it. In no time at all you are going to see a vast improvement on your work.

Chapter 2 – Making Your First Mark For Real

In the last chapter, I told you how to get started. Now, I want you to take that to the next level and start writing a work of art. I don't want you to get discouraged on the outset of this. It is going to take you time and effort to get to where you want to be, so your early work is going to look like a beginner did it.

The more you work at it, the better it is going to be, and the sooner you are going to be able to make things that look professional. So I encourage you to keep up the good work, and to practice practice practice.

You will need a guide

For your first piece, I want you to come off of the lined paper and use blank paper, but I want you to keep a guide so you know where you are supposed to be. You can do this with a ruler and light pencil marks that can later be erased, or you can do it on regular lined paper (such as notebook paper).

Choose the font you are going to use, and get in the proper position. Make sure you are holding your pen properly, and that you are sitting up straight. Dip your pen in the ink, and you are ready to begin.

Practice the lettering

For your beginning piece, it is likely that you are going to have to go over your letters several times before you are able to make some that you are happy with. Now, I am not saying that you can't be happy with what you are doing in the beginning, but you do need to get to where your work looks professional no matter where you are doing it.

You can make the same letter several times on this new, unlined paper, or you can try making words. Either way, you are going to have to work on this for a while to get the hang of how large you want your letters to be, and keeping them in a straight line.

A lot of beginning writers find that they have issues with their letters trailing down the page as they go along. This is a result of poor posture, as well as not holding the pen properly. If you sit up straight, pull your shoulders back, and hold your pen the right way, you are going to have a much easier time making your lines stay straight.

Work your words and your letters over and over until they start to come naturally. This could happen in a few hours, or it could take a few days. We all learn at our own pace, so don't be hard on yourself. You are going to get there if you try.

Put it all together

This whole world of doing the same letter over and over is bound to get tiresome for you. I am sure you are thinking of the days when you were in grade school and were learning the letters for the first time. You had to trace the letters, then you had to form words, then came the sentences.

Calligraphy is much the same way, only you now have an advantage because you know what you are shooting for with your letters. You will notice, no matter what kind of font you are using, the letters all look pretty close to what they look like in normal English. This is going to give you an advantage when you are trying to learn how to form them in calligraphy style.

When you are used to how they are formed, you are going to feel them come naturally to you. The way you struggle right now is going to fade with time, and it is going to look as beautiful as you have pictured in your head. Little steps is the key to bigger steps.

The letters first, then the words, then the whole script. Keep them going in the proper line, and you are going to see them come together in the proper way.

Chapter 3 – Adding that Personal Touch

You more than likely have noticed that calligraphy is so much more than just a bunch of big letters. There are dashes, swooshes, swoops, and all kinds of little dots here and there.

In and of themselves, they don't look like they belong, but when you take a step back and look at the entire piece, you can see quite clearly that they do. You may be surprised to learn that these marks aren't all meant to form the letters, but that some marks are just a personal touch that was added in by the artist.

That's right, you can make your own style of lettering that is personal to you if you so choose. In the beginning, we are going to look at how you can do this the proper way, following a guide, but then I am going to show you how you can make them your own.

In no time, you are going to be making your own script that is personal to only you, and if it catches on, it is going to be a font that many people are going to want to use.

But for now, let's start with the basic tricks of the trade.

Dashes and Marks

Dashes and marks are small points that appear in the script, and they can be just about anywhere, depending on the font you are using. You will notice in your own particular font the letters that have the dashes and dots, and you are going to have to learn how to add them in.

It is important to note in calligraphy that you need to place the dashes and dots in where they belong. You can't do 'close enough' with this and expect it all to turn out. Follow the guide you are using and pay special attention to where the marks are on the page, and learn to do them yourself.

This is going to be tedious and time consuming at first, but it is going to be well worth your while when you are able to do it as second nature.

Swirls and Swoops

The swirls and swoops are placed at the beginning and end of the entire script. You are going to notice that some letters have small swirls to them anyway, and that is fine, but you are also going to see that these are much larger at the beginning and end of the script.

This is because you are going to sort of greet and end the conversation with these letters. You are going to give a lot of emphasis to both the beginning and end words with the initial and end swirls, but keep in mind that they still need to be modest.

Look at your guide. You are going to notice that a lot of the letters don't have these elaborate swirls, and that is because they are meant for you to use them in common writing. If you were to put them in a letter, you would need to add in these bigger swirls yourself.

You could look up beginning and end letter marks online if you wanted to, or you could just do it yourself. There isn't a wrong way to do this once you know the basic script, and this is where your artist can break forth and leave his mark on the page.

Making it your own

I know that when you are in the beginning of anything, you are worried that you are going to do it wrong, so you are a lot more likely to follow the things to the letter. This is the right way to do it at first for sure, but I want to assure you that you can't do it wrong if you are expressing yourself.

You are going to learn how to do the lettering at first, but then you are allowed to make it your own. Add in your own swoops and swirls, dashes, and marks. You are an artist, and calligraphy is an art.

Do what you think looks right, and what best expresses yourself. If you want it bigger, go bigger, if you want to keep it calm, go with the soft and sweet. With practice, you are going to learn how to make the letters properly, so that is going to be second nature.

Once that happens, you are free to do whatever you need to make it your own. As long as the letters are legible and look like you want them to by the time you are done, then you are doing it right.

Chapter 4 – The Wonderful World of Cards

Most people associate calligraphy with cards. They think of greeting cards, wedding announcements, graduation announcements, and even business cards. When you are writing in this kind of way, the two just seem to go hand in hand.

You are going to have a major advantage when you are able to make these cards yourself, you aren't going to have to pay extra to get that font that you want, and you won't have to stress about finding that one perfect card at the supermarket anymore.

There are a few tips and tricks that you need to keep in mind, however, depending on the card that you are making, but don't worry, I am going to help you learn what they are.

In no time at all you are going to be able to make your own kind of card, no matter what it is you need to say.

Greeting Cards

Greeting cards are likely the easiest of the cards to make. You have to think of what you are going to say, then say it in the space that you have. The key points that you need to remember are to use paper that doesn't bleed the ink, and to put the background on first.

If you are going to paste the words into the card, you want to write them out before you put them into the card, if you make a mistake you are going to be better able to fix it this way.

If you are writing over a faded background, make sure you write out what you want to say as practice first, then do it on the card. If you do happen to make a mistake, don't panic, you can fix it or you can start again, but it is always better if you can do it without making a mistake in the first place.

Place Cards

Next on the list we have place cards. These are seen in weddings, parties, or anywhere that you need to indicate who needs to sit where. If you are in a smaller gathering, it is likely you can get away with using initials only.

If you are doing this, then you can use all of the swoops and swirls that you need, but if you are going to be using the entire name of the guest, make sure that it is easily legible for them to read.

There is nothing worse than guests not knowing what to do because they can't read your writing! Make sure you use dark ink on a light back, or a light glitter on a dark back.

The easier you can make this for your guests, while embracing your elegance, the better off you are going to be in the long run. Remember to always use paper that doesn't bleed the ink, and if you are pasting your paper onto the backing, then you should write the name or the initials before you paste onto the card.

Creativity is free to flow, but make sure you always keep that margin for error.

Invitations

When it comes to invitations, the front can be a lot more elaborate than the information itself. Use your finest and grandest calligraphy to get the main point across, then use a smaller and more to the point font to fill in the details.

It is best to make invitations with the greeting and main message on the front, with the details inside. This is going to give you plenty of room for your creativity on the outside, while you can be short and to the point on the inside.

Use the paper that won't bleed the ink, and always write on the paper before you paste it to the backing. Remember that your invite is going to stay a lot nicer if you mail it in an envelope as well. Many people like to use their skills on postcard style invites, but I recommend you put it in an envelope to ensure that your work isn't damaged in the mail.

You never know what could happen with travel!

Business Cards

Business cards are a little tricky to handle with calligraphy, but if you are careful, you can pull off a beautiful card that will catch the eye of any customer.

For starters, you know that you are going to need paper that doesn't bleed, and that you need to write on paper that you are going to paste to the card. This doesn't necessarily apply to business cards, as they are a lot less decorated, but as it is your business, you can do what you want.

Another thing to keep in mind is that you are only going to make one, then have copies made of that one. You don't need to do all of the cards by hand, and you want consistency, so one is enough.

Make the name of the business in the finest hand, then the details in a clearly legible script underneath. You don't want to get too elaborate in the detail script because at the size it is going to be, you are going to want it to be as clear as possible.

Use the elaborate swirls on the front of the lettering only, when you are doing a business card, you don't want to overdue the fancy look because you want customers to get to the point.

Practice for a few of them, and see what you like. When you are happy with the font, print it up and send it out.

Cards are personal items that you can have a lot of fun with. You are given a lot of freedom with how they look, and you can make them say whatever you want. Just make sure that you use paper that doesn't bleed, and that your words are legible, and you have all of the freedom in the world!

Chapter 5 – Next Steps

I can't emphasize enough how important it is for you to practice. You need to use this skill for more than just a few minutes a day if you are going to get better at it, and you are going to need to work at what you do know if you want to keep it going.

Take care of your tools

As with any trade, you are going to need to take care of the tools. Clean your pen and your ink well. Keep track of your notebooks and your items. Replace old or broken tips and don't let your ink get gummy around the top.

It isn't fun to clean these things, but your pen and ink is going to stay so much nicer in the long run if you do, and your letters are going to reflect your care.

Keep track of your skills

Save your old work so you can look back and see how far you have come. There is no shame in what you do in the beginning, just move forward. It is fun to look back over the years and see how far you have come, especially from your first letter to where you are now.

Learn new things

Don't ever settle at good enough. You need to keep learning, and keep practicing to make yourself better than you are today. Don't ever assume that you are the master at what you are doing, or that you don't need to keep learning. Don't be hard on yourself, but never settle for where you are right now, either.

Onward and upward, let that be the goal of all of your writing.

Review the old

Just like you need to keep track of your progress, you also need to practice what you have already learned. The skills that you don't use in writing often, make a point of going back and learning those over again, and reviewing them.

The more you are able to incorporate regular practice into what you are doing, the sharper your skills are going to become. Keep in mind also that the more skills you are good at, the easier it is going to be to learn new skills.

Find support and help, and have fun

Get a group together, and have fun. This isn't an easy hobby to do by yourself, especially if you are around people that don't understand. Find friends or other people that are into the hobby and are willing to help you practice and learn. The best way to learn anything is to have people around you that are going to work at it with you. The more the merrier! Help each other with the tough things, and have fun with the easy things.

The more you work together, the faster you are going to see yourself get better at it.

Express yourself!

This is a form of communication, and it is a skill, but above all, it is an art. You are going to have all kinds of freedom with this hobby, and you should take advantage of that.

Express yourself, make it your own. The more fun you have with it, the more personal it is going to be. You are going to love how you can personalize anything from now on, and rest assured that you can't do it wrong.

Have fun and take care of your items, and practice what you have learned. You are going to be a great writer in no time.

Happy writing!

Conclusion

There you have it, everything that you need to know to get started in the wonderful art of calligraphy. The next thing you need to do is to practice, and stick with it even when you are feeling frustrated or like you can't do it.

Practice is the key to success in calligraphy. It takes a steady hand and a sure stroke to give the letters their definition and beauty, and if you are going to become good at giving that stroke, you are going to need to practice.

These things aren't natural, but they do come to those that are willing to put in the time and effort into what they are doing. If you get the proper equipment, and you are willing to work at it, then you are going to find that your work is every bit as good as what you see in the stores, if not better because you can make it personal.

There is an inner artist in all of us, and more often than not it just needs a little push to get out into the open and make the most of the talent that is inside. I am going to help you push your talent into the open, and help you see what your potential and capabilities are.

There is a circle you are going to break in to. The better you get at this, the more fun it is going to be, so you are going to want to do it more, and the more you do it, the better you will get at it.

Don't let another day go by without you at least starting out with your new art.

Good things come to those who work for it, and it is well worth your effort.